How to Register

ISBNs

&

Copyrights

How To For You

MercerPublications.com

Books and eBooks for
Authors, Improving writers
and Independent
publishers

ISBN 13: 978-1-52381-514-2

Read what other authors had to say about the How to For You Series of books for independent authors.

"A concise and extremely well-written guide like this one by Dorothy May Mercer is exactly what every aspiring author needs."

"This guide is clear, concise, and full of useful information."

"This book gives you exactly what you need to get the job done and is written so that you totally understand - it's not Greek. A must have for the self-publisher! FIVE STARS!"

"Thank you, Dorothy Mercer, for writing such a wonderful, greatly needed concise book."

"Simple to follow and easy to quickly implement. Dorothy writes the perfect how-to."

"...a must-have for indie writers - especially those who have not yet gone through the process to discover all the pitfalls by stumbling into them themselves. Spend a dollar now and save yourself hours of frustration."

"I have been looking for a book like this one. Concise and well written in language easily understandable by the beginner all the way to someone with some experience."

"I picked this one up because I've read a lot of the author's fiction books and was really impressed with her style and story-telling skills."

The Complete *How to For You* Series:

How to Write Sentences and Paragraphs

How to Design & Format Your Paragraphs

How to Format Your Book, *for Publishing*

How to Write Great Dialog, *Your Book Needs This*

How to Write Fiction

How to Edit a Book, *With a Friend*

How to Fix Errors in Your Document *Find and Replace Easily*

How to Add an Interactive Table of Contents

How to Install a Link in Your Document

How to Prepare Your Book for Kindle

How to Design a Kindle eBook Cover

How to Install Your Kindle Cover on Print Books, *and Vice Versa*

How to Sell Your eBook Using Amazon Free Days

How to Use Your Books for Free Ads

How to Market Your Book, *Marketing 101*

How to Register ISBNs & Copyrights

How to Get an Audible Version, *of Your Book*

How to Create a Picture Book

How to Self-Publish

Bargain Bundles:

Marketing Bundle 2-4-1

Marketing Bundle 3-4-1

Cover Designing Bundle

Formatting Bundle 2-4-1

For prices and ordering information please copy the address or hold down ctrl & click below:

www.MercerPublications.com

www.Amazon.com/   Search for Dorothy May Mercer

How to Register ISBNs & Copyrights

How to For You #19

This book will answer your questions:

Where do I get an ISBN number for my book?

Must I always get an ISBN number?

What will it cost?

Is it worth the trouble to copyright my book?

What does copyrighting cost?

How long will it take?

What is the easiest way to do it?

What changes have occurred since Createspace went out of business?

Does a US copyright protect me in other countries?

Where do I go to obtain international copyrights?

New: How do I get a Library of Congress control number?

Table of Contents

Part One

ISBN Numbers

Chapter 1 What is an ISBN number?

The **International Standard Book Number** (**ISBN**) is a unique numeric commercial book identifier.

An ISBN is assigned to each edition and variation (except re-printings) of a book. For example, an e-book, a paperback and a hardcover edition of the same book would each have a different ISBN. The ISBN is 13 digits long if assigned on or after 1 January 2007, and 10 digits long if assigned before 2007. The method of assigning an ISBN is nation-based and varies from country to country, often depending on how large the publishing industry is within a country.

Occasionally, a book may appear without a printed ISBN if it is printed privately or the author does not follow the usual ISBN procedure; however, this can be rectified later.

Today's ISBN is 13 digits long and consists of 5 parts, separated by a hyphen.

- EAN (*prefix element*) meaning country.
- Group *(registration group)* according to language or territory.
- Publisher *(registrant)*.
- Title *(publication)*.
- Check digit..

A 13-digit ISBN will be separated into its parts (*prefix element*, *registration group*, *registrant*, *publication* and *check digit*). When this is done it is customary to separate the parts with <u>hyphens</u> or spaces. Figuring out how to correctly separate a given ISBN number is complicated, because most of the parts do not use a fixed number of digits.

Chapter 2 How ISBNs Are Issued

ISBN issuance is country-specific, in that ISBNs are issued by the ISBN registration agency that is responsible for that country or territory regardless of the publication language. The ranges of ISBNs assigned to any particular country are based on the publishing profile of the country concerned, and so the ranges will vary depending on the number of books and the number, type, and size of publishers that are active.

Some ISBN registration agencies are based in national libraries or within ministries of culture and thus may receive direct funding from government to support their services.

In other cases, the ISBN registration service is provided by organizations such as bibliographic data providers that are not government funded.

In Canada, ISBNs are issued at no cost with the stated purpose of encouraging Canadian culture.

In the United Kingdom, United States, and some other countries, where the service is provided by non-government-funded organisations, the issuing of ISBNs requires payment of a fee.

Chapter 3 eISBN

Only the term "ISBN" should be used. The terms "eISBN" and "e-ISBN" have historically been sources of confusion and should be avoided.

If a book exists in one or more digital (e-book) formats, each of those formats must have its own ISBN. In other words, each of the three separate EPUB, Amazon Kindle, and PDF formats of a particular book will have its own specific ISBN. They should not share the ISBN of the paper version, and there is no generic "eISBN" which encompasses all the e-book formats for a title.

ISBN Users Manual

The latest edition of the Users' Manual is now available in 13 languages: **Albanian, Arabic, Chinese (Mandarin), Dutch, English, Estonian, French, German, Hungarian, Portuguese, Serbian, Slovene** and **Spanish**.

In addition, a translation of the fifth edition of the Manual (with some updates about digital publications) is available in **Danish** and a translation of the 2007 edition of the Manual is available in **Persian.**

- See more at: https://www.isbn-international.org/

Chapter 4 Locate International Issuers

You can find a list of international agencies at: https://www.isbn-international.org/agencies. Some of the common ones are listed below:

Australia: ISBNs are issued by the commercial library services agency Thorpe-Bowker, and prices range from $42 for a single ISBN (plus a $55 registration fee for new publishers) to $2,890 for a block of 1,000 ISBNs. Access is immediate when requested via their website.

Canada: Library and Archives Canada, a government agency, is responsible for issuing ISBNs, and there is no cost. Works in French are issued an ISBN by the Bibliothèque et Archives nationales du Québec.

India: The Raja Rammohun Roy Library Foundation (RRRLF), part of the Ministry of Culture, is responsible for registration of Indian publishers, authors, universities, institutions, and government departments that are responsible for publishing books.

Italy: The privately held company *EDISER srl*, owned by *Associazione Italiana Editori* (Italian Publishers Association) is responsible for issuing ISBNs. The original national prefix 978-88 is reserved for publishing companies, starting at €49 for a ten-codes block while a new prefix 979-12 is dedicated to self-publishing authors, at a fixed price of €25 for a single code.

Pakistan: The <u>National Library of Pakistan</u> is responsible for ISBN registrations for Pakistani publishers, authors, universities, institutions, and government departments that are responsible for publishing books.

South Africa: The <u>National Library of South Africa</u> is responsible for ISBN issuance for South African publishing institutions and authors.

United Kingdom and Republic of Ireland: The privately held company *Nielsen Book Services Ltd*, part of <u>Nielsen Holdings</u> N.V., is responsible for issuing ISBNs in blocks of 10, 100 or 1000. Prices start from £120 (plus <u>VAT</u>) for the smallest block on a standard turnaround of ten days.

United States: In the United States, the privately held company <u>R.R. Bowker</u> issues ISBNs. There is a charge that varies depending upon the number of ISBNs purchased, with prices starting at $125.00 for a single number. Access is immediate when requested via their website.

Chapter 5 Can Someone Else Sell Me a Number?

The short answer is "No." The numbers are assigned to the original purchaser, whether that be a publisher, group, or an individual author.

Nevertheless, entities may buy a group of numbers and then "assign" them to individual buyers for a fee, or for free. There is nothing wrong with this.

Just understand that the registrant will be the entity from which you purchased the number. This registrant will be identified by the third set of numbers in a 13 digit ISBN.

For example the number 62329 identifies my company, "Mercer Publications & Ministries, Inc." as this is the way I registered that group of numbers.

Whenever I publish a book for another author, I "assign" one of Mercer Pub's numbers to that book.

My task is to go online to Bowkerlink.com (the U.S. agency) and enter all of the information about that book, including the author, title, price, cover and many other details. The third set of numbers in the 13-digit ISBN will identify that exact book and none other.

Ways to avoid buying a number.

Well, the easiest way to avoid having to pay for a number is to be lucky enough to be born a Canadian. In that case, the numbers are free. For the rest of us, the only way that I know is to obtain an "assigned" number from our publisher or printer.

For example, some publishers own a group of numbers which they assign to books for free. Other publishers may charge, of course. For example, Mercer Publications purchased a block of 1000 numbers which we assign, in order, as we publish new books and new editions of books.

Some companies offer a variety of services for which they charge. Along with that, they may offer free ISBN numbers from the stock of numbers which they own. For example, Kindle Direct Publishing (KDP.com), the publishing arm of Amazon.com, offers the option of providing your own number or using one of theirs.

CreateSpace Former Publishing Arm of Amazon

Before they were absorbed by KDP, CreateSpace published thousands of books with free numbers. Those authors who took advantage of that may now be alarmed to find their books transferred to Kindle Direct Publishing. There is no need to panic. KDP supports the CreateSpace numbers. They are still listed with Bowkerlink. Even though CreateSpace is out of business, the numbers live on. The author merely has to complete a few steps to republish the book with KDP, using the same number.

However, not all publishers have such a cozy relationship with Amazon. Therefore, if an independent publisher goes out of business, it might be necessary to re-publish those books with new ISBN numbers and a new publisher.

For more information please see my book, How to Self-Publish.Your Book.

Chapter 6 Here's a Trick—a Balancing Act

Can you imagine an instance where you, an author, might publish the exact same printed book with two different ISBN numbers? I have learned to do just that with all of my print books and here is why: It is a balancing act between price and percentage of royalty.

As you may know, up until they transferred to KDP.Amazon, I had used CreateSpace to print my books. Those of you who used this service realize that there was a vast difference in royalties, depending on the seller(s) you chose to distribute your book..

The percent of royalty earned in these six different outlets ranged from very low to medium, and depended on cost of printing and the price you set, yourself.

For example, one of my books was priced at $10.95. If Amazon sold the book, I received $2.82, or 25.75% of the retail price. However, if the book was sold through one of CreateSpace's Expanded Distribution outlets, I received a paltry $.63 (sixty-three cents.) or 5.7% return.

And so, for Expanded Distribution purposes, I published a second book at a higher price, in order to maximize the royalty from those sales.

However, as you know, there is a price point beyond which there will be fewer and fewer buyers willing to pay. After all, the competition is fierce. And so, it became a balancing act.

The neat thing about Createspace was they allowed me to issue two editions with different prices, one for Amazon and one for Expanded Distribution. I could select which ones I wanted. The CreateSpace service representative suggested to me they could print two versions of my book, one with their ISBN number and one with my own number. Since then, I did exactly that. The only difference between the two versions was the price and the ISBN number. I used the CreateSpace ISBN number for copies I wished to assign to "Expanded Distribution," at a higher price, and my own ISBN number for copies I wished to market on Amazon, at a "user-friendly" price. I tried to set prices that would garner about the same royalty from either seller.

Unfortunately, as of this writing, the new Kindle Direct Publishing for print books, does not allow that option. I must sell on Amazon, first, and then I may select Expanded Distribution, as well. But it must be the same book. I cannot have a KDP book that is only for Expanded Distribution and not on Amazon. Maybe I could try having the same book at two different prices, designating only the higher priced one for Expanded Distribution, but I would have both books on Amazon at the two different prices. I'm not sure that is worth the trouble. Instead I have looked for a different solution. More on that later.

KDP.Amazon Pricing

For your information, here is how the new pricing system works:

KDP allows a 60% royalty for Amazon's printed book sales and 40% for Expanded Distribution. At first glance that looks fabulous, does it not? However, the percentage does not take into account the cost of printing. First the royalty of 60% is figured on the retail price which you set yourself. From that the cost of printing is subtracted.

Let us take, for example, the book I mentioned earlier at $10.95. Multiply that by 60% and you get a lovely $6.57. Sounds great. However, after you subtract the cost of printing, it loses its punch. Supposing you elect Expanded distribution. Now the royalty becomes $4.38, minus the cost of printing. Suddenly, the cost of printing looms large in one's thinking. Maybe those extra white spaces I put in my books are not so important after all.

Another issue is that the author cannot assume the books have been put on expanded distribution at all. Of the eighty or so books that were transferred from CreateSpace to Kiindle

Direct Publishing, about half had been on The

Selecting **Expanded Distribution**

I discovered, to my dismay that the Expanded Distribution designation did not always automatically carry over from Createspace to KDP. I had to go into the file and check each one manually.

And so, while I am keeping my books on Kindle Direct Publishing, I am also using another outlet to help me with Expanded Distribution.

Lightning Source (subsidiary of Ingram) allows me to the flexibility to set one price and then discount it to various outlets. It was important to me to have my books available on Baker and Taylor and Ingram. Why? Because the librarians upon whom I call, purchase their stock from one or the other, mostly from Baker and Taylor. I learned that the reason they do this is because Baker and Taylor and Ingram each give them a discount.

I tried to get my books on B & T directly with no success. Although I am an independent publisher, they only list those publishers who sold books in the uber-thousands, (translation: the big N.Y. giants).

Librarians who purchase my book(s) through Baker & Taylor or Ingram will be getting a discount, so there is no harm done. I have been pleasantly surprised at the business I get through that outlet.

Part Two

Copyrights

Chapter 7 Copyrights

It is easy to find information about copyrighting online. One of the best articles is reprinted as follows, from WikiHow.com, where you can find how to do many things.

"When you've created something original, such as a book, you want to ensure that your work–whether published or unpublished–is protected. Contrary to popular belief, sending yourself a copy of your work through certified mail is not an adequate means of obtaining copyright. Copyrighting your work through common law is a way of proving that the work is your own, but official registration is necessary before you have any power to take action against someone who is stealing or profiting from your work.

"Fix the date of your copyright.

"This will protect you should there be a legal ownership dispute in the future. There are several informal ways to solidify your claim without pursuing official registration, though there is no provision in copyright law regarding these methods:

- Publish your work to gain common law copyright protection. Whether you publish on a blog, a newspaper, a magazine, or in book form, this is another method to establish you as the original author.

- Be sure that when published, the work contains your full name and the date of publication.

- Note that if you are a US citizen, you will need to officially register with the US Copyright Office before you are able to make a claim in a US court (even if you already own a right on your work). Registration may also entitle you to statutory damages in a US legal system.

"Use the copyright symbol.

"According to applicable law in most countries, you own the copyright in the work as soon as it is fixed in a readable format. By placing the copyright symbol (©) on your work, you are telling others that you know your rights, [as well as establishing] a legally-relevant date of original publication.

- "You might also consider adding reference to the legislation that backs up your copyright claim, such as: "© 2013, [your name]. Except as provided by the Copyright Act [date, etc.] no part of this publication may be reproduced, stored in a retrieval system or transmitted in any form or by any means without the prior written permission of the publisher."

- "The appropriate wording is not set in stone and is often defined by your publisher's preference, or by jurisdictional tradition, so ask your publisher or attorney for advice.

- "If you are considering publishing in various countries, it is a good idea to ask your publisher's legal team or your own attorney about the value of registering in all countries where your works will be published."

Chapter 8 Applying for US Copyrights

Applying Online

For you reasonably tech-savvy folks, the easier, cheaper and faster way to apply for a copyright is online.

In the United States the average processing time for e-filing (eCO) is generally, about eight months, whereas paper filing can take up to eighteen months.

Which browsers does eCO support?

The eCO System has been confirmed for use with the Firefox browser on the Microsoft Windows 7 Operating system. Hopefully they will be updating to Windows 8, 10 and beyond, soon.

What payment options are available in eCO?

You may pay with credit/debit card or ACH transfer via Pay.gov or with a copyright office deposit account.

The internet address of the US Government Copyright Office is www.copyright.gov. From here you can access much information and many helps. If you choose to mail your application, one is available here for downloading.

If you choose to make your application online, choose the eCO button: "Log in to eCO". Follow the instructions to open an account and pay the processing fee with a credit card or personal account, at Pay.gov.

What is Pay.gov?

Pay.gov is a secure, web-based application operated by the U.S. Treasury Department that allows users to make online payments to government agencies by credit card or by debit from a checking or savings account.

Do I have to create a user account with Pay.gov?

No. For payment via credit/debit card or ACH transfer, eCO will forward you directly to the Pay.gov payment screen. Once payment has been completed, Pay.gov will redirect you back into eCO to complete your registration. You will receive a payment confirmation email from Pay.gov after a successful transaction.

What is a deposit account?

To save time, frequent users may opt to open a deposit account.

The Copyright Office maintains a system of deposit accounts for those who frequently use its services. An individual or firm may establish a deposit account, make advance deposits into that account, and charge copyright fees against the balance in their account via eCO.

How do I upload an electronic copy of my work in eCO?

When payment is complete, you will see the "Payment Successful" screen, and follow these directions: (If not, refer to the Troubleshooting section).

1. Click the "Continue" button on the upper right of the Payment Successful screen.

2. Click the green "Select files to upload" button in the "Deposit Submission" table. A window with fields for browsing on your computer and selecting files to be uploaded should appear.

3. Select the file(s) to be uploaded for the work being registered. As they are selected, the file names will be displayed under the green "Select Files to upload" button.

4. After selecting all files for the work, click the blue "Start Upload" button.

5. When all files have been uploaded for the work, click the green "Complete Your Submission" button.

6. If you submitted multiple applications together, repeat these steps for each application to upload an electronic copy of the work(s).

Use the correct browser

The copyright system is set up to use the Firefox browser, with Windows 7.

Other browsers such as Internet Explorer, Chrome, Safari and Netscape (as well as out-of-date browsers) may work, but potentially could show less than optimal behavior when used with the eCO system.

Do I need to configure my browser before using eCO?

Yes. Before getting started be sure to check your browser's settings and make the following adjustments as necessary:

Disable your browser's pop-up blocker. Disable any 3rd party toolbars (e.g., Google or Yahoo Toolbar). Set your security and privacy settings to MEDIUM.

Processing Paper Forms:

The US website states to expect processing time to be generally, up to 13 months.

Applications forms can be downloaded from the Copyright Office web site. In the US If you apply by mail, send an application, fee, and deposit copy or copies to:

Library of Congress Copyright Office

101 Independence Avenue SE

Washington, DC 20559

This address differs from the address for opening and maintaining a deposit account. Use the deposit account address only for opening or replenishing the deposit account.

For Further Information

Circulars, announcements, regulations, other related materials, and all copyright application forms are available on the Copyright Office website at www.copyright.gov. To send an email communication, click on Contact Us at the bottom of the homepage.

By Telephone: For general information about copyright, call the Copyright Public Information Office at (202) 707-3000 or 1-877-476- 0778 (toll free). Staff members are on duty from 8:30 am to 5:00 pm, Eastern Time, Monday through Friday, except federal holidays. Recorded information is available 24 hours a day. Or, if you know which application forms and circulars you want, request them 24 hours a day from the Forms and Publications Hotline at (202) 707-9100. Leave a recorded message. By Regular Mail Write to:

Library of Congress Copyright Office-PUB

101 Independence Avenue SE

Washington, DC 20559

What are the US Copyright Fees?

The current fee is **$35** for filing a copyright registration online for single authors (not joint authors), single works (not collections) and for works that are not a work made for hire.

All other works will cost **$55** to file online. Filing a paper form is currently **$85.**

Chapter 9 International Copyrights

Original works of expression that are eligible for copyright protection are protected under national copyright laws. Protection against unauthorized use in a particular country depends on the national laws of that country; in other words, copyright protection depends on the national laws where protection is sought.

International copyright conventions and treaties have been developed to establish obligations for treaty member countries to adhere to and implement in their national laws, thus providing more certainty and understanding about the levels of copyright protection in particular countries. Understanding which works by which authors from which countries may be eligible for copyright protection in the target country has been simplified by countries joining international copyright treaties and conventions.

There is no such thing as an "international copyright" that will automatically protect an author's writings throughout the world. The United States is a member of many treaties and conventions affecting copyright, including the Berne Convention for the Protection of Literary and Artistic Works; the World Intellectual Property Organization (WIPO) Copyright Treaty; the WIPO Performances and Phonograms Treaty; the Geneva Convention for the Protection of Producers of Phonograms Against Unauthorized Duplication of Their Phonograms; the Brussels Convention Relating to the Distribution of Program-Carrying Signals Transmitted by Satellite; and the Universal Copyright Convention.

Recent developments have resulted in two new WIPO copyright treaties: the Beijing Treaty on Audiovisual Performances and the Marrakesh Treaty to Facilitate Access to Published Works for Persons Who Are Blind, Visually Impaired, or Otherwise Print Disabled. Neither of these two new treaties has entered into force, and the

United States has not yet deposited its instruments of ratification with WIPO.

In addition to international treaties and conventions, other instruments, such as trade agreements, require member countries to comply with specific obligations. The World Trade Organization (WTO) administers the Agreement on Trade-Related Aspects of Intellectual Property Rights (TRIPS), which contains obligations related to intellectual property rights, including copyright and enforcement measures, in the context of a multilateral trade agreement.

Building on TRIPS standards, free trade agreements concluded by the United States require the parties to have robust copyright laws and enforcement measures. Circular 38a provides more details on the international conventions, treaties, and other bilateral instruments that the United States has concluded with other countries, and it details the participation of other countries in these same instruments. The Copyright Office's website contains links to all the relevant copyright conventions and treaties.

If you seek copyright protection for your U.S. work in another country, it is important to determine the points of attachment under that country's copyright system. If possible, do so before your work is published anywhere, because protection may depend on the facts existing at the time of first publication. The scope of protection available in that country will then turn on the substantive provisions available under that country's law and practice. Keep in mind, however, that some countries offer little or no copyright protection to foreign works. Specific facts, circumstances, and national laws are important in any international copyright analysis.

For more information on the scope of copyright protection provided by other countries, you may want to consult a legal expert familiar with foreign and U.S. copyright laws. The U.S. Copyright Office is not permitted to recommend attorneys or agents to give legal advice on foreign or domestic laws.

Chapter 10   Where to go for Other Countries

It is important to go to the official registration site in the particular country. Why? Because it is easy to mistakenly go to a private site who will charge you an extra fee to do the very thing that you can do yourself.

Here are a few of the more common addresses:

Canada

http://www.ic.gc.ca/eic/site/cipointernet-internetopic.nsf/eng/h_wr00003.html

United Kingdom

https://www.gov.uk/government/organisations/intellectual-property-office

Australia

http://www.ipaustralia.gov.au/

Each country has its own unique web site. Usually a search of YourCountry.gov.copyright/

will turn up a list of appropriate sites. If that doesn't work, try entering a question in the search area such are, Where is the official copyright site for [My country]?

Part Three

Library of Congress Control Numbers

Chapter 11 The Library of Congress (LOC)

The United States Library of Congress, located in Washington D.C. is an enormous establishment situated in several buildings and covering some city blocks. Huge as it is, personal service is still available to authors.

This is the ultimate library for authors who feel the need to preserve their works forever and for researchers who, hundreds of years from now, wish to look up their ancestors. It also facilitates cataloging and other book processing activities for libraries and book sellers who obtain copies of the book. Although filing your book with the LOC is a nice thing to do, it is merely an option—not required or necessary, unless you expect or hope to sell thousands of copies to libraries, book stores and other institutions.

If you are living in the US, or are an American living elsewhere, you have the option of filing your books with the LOC (Library of Congress) CIP (Cataloging in Publication) Program.

For a new book you will go through an application process, filing first an electronic and later a final printed paper copy of your book.

Once you complete the application process you will receive the LOC Control Number, which can be published in your book's opening pages, along with the other credits such as ISBN number, publisher and copyright date.

Certain books are not eligible, such as books in non-Western Eutopean languages and books consisting mainly of images, tables, charts or mathematical or chemical formulas, etc.

How Do I Open a New Account?

First you must open a new account.

To obtain CIP data, you must first complete the application to participate and obtain an account nuumber and password. All of your pending and future books may be filed with that account. In about one week the LOC will correspond with you by email, advising you when each step is processed.

The account number and password provide access to the form for requesting CIP data. A JavaScript-enabled browser such as Mozilla Firefox or Microsoft Explorer is required to complete the application and submition forms.

It takes about a week for the LOC to process your application to open a new account. Upon approval, you will be notified by email of your new account number.

Next you must enter your online account and fill out an application for a LOC Control Number for any book that you are publishing. You must complete a CIP data application and transmit the full text or core required materials for each title. There are exact instructions on the site telling you how to attach and transmit the text in US-ASCII with line breaks.

In WordPerfect you select "ASCII DOS Text (.txt)" from the list of file types—not WordPerfect (.wpd).

In Microsoft Word you select "MS-DOS Text with line breaks (.txt)"–not Word document (.doc or .docx).

The clerk uses this text to catalog your book and issue a LOC Control number. Later this text is deleted, after they receive the printed book showing the number on the copyright page.

It is of utmost importance to send a perfected final paper copy to the LOC as soon as possible after publication. Failure to do this may result in cancelation of your priveleges. That mailing address is:

Library of Congress
US Programs, Law and Literature Division
Cataloging in Publication Program
101 Independence Avenue, S.E.
Washington, DC 20540-4283

The complimentary copy is required to verify the accuracy of the CIP record and provide additional information, such as number of pages, not available at the time the CIP data is created.

So far, the instructions have been for unpublished books which are in the process of being published, not for cataloging your already published books.

Can I Get Cataloging for a Book Which is Already Published?

All works submitted to the Copyright Office to meet copyright obligations are also reviewed by Library of Congress selection librarians. Works selected for addition to the Library's collections are assigned a cataloging priority and are cataloged according to that priority. The Library does not provide current status reports for individual works processed in this manner. The LOC database, however, is available via the Internet (http://catalog.loc.gov) where you can search for your copyrighted works to determine whether they have been cataloged.

According to the LOC website, owners of published works should consider working with a professional librarian at a local library to obtain cataloging.

Bibliography

Portions of this book have been excerpted, paraphrased and referenced from the following e-publications:

https://www.isbn-international.org/

www.wikihow.com

www.copyright.gov

www.createspace.com

https://www.myidentifiers.com/get-your-isbn-now

http://bowkerlink.com/

http://www.loc.gov/publish/pcn/

If you found this book useful, we would be ever so grateful if you would post a positive review.   *Thank you very much.*

Dorothy May Mercer

Dear Reader.

Was this article helpful to you? Did it deliver as promised? If you liked this book, please do me favors:

- Please go to Amazon and leave a simple, but nice, four or five-star review. Go to any/all of these sites and search for Dorothy May Mercer
- Thanks a million.
-

  - US Amazon.com/
      (Search for Dorothy May Mercer)
  - UK: Amazon.co.UK (Search for Dorothy May Mercer)
  - CA: Amazon.com.ca (Search for Dorothy May Mercer
  - AU: Amazon.com.au (Search for Dorothy May Mercer

In return, a bonus gift for you, just for reading this book.

Go to MercerPublications.com and scroll down to Short & Fun Stories:

For your free E book gift, please go to MercerPublications.com and click on the title, "Short & Fun Stories."

And while you are there please consider another book or booklet by this author.

The complete "How to For You" series of booklets for improving writers.

  1. "How to Write Sentences and Paragraphs" *in Your Novel*

2. "How to Install a Link in Your Document"

3. "How to Sell Your eBook Using Amazon Free Days"

4. "How to Prepare Your Book for Kindle"

5. "How to Fix Errors in Your Document," *Find and Replace Globally*

6. "How to Use Your Book for Free Ads"

7. "How to Design and Format Your Paragraphs"

8. "How to Design a Kindle eBook Cover"

9. "How to Install Your Kindle Cover on Print Books," *and Vice Versa*

10. "How to Add an Interactive Table of Contents"

11. "How to Format Your Book, for Publishing"—*Two Editions, Ebook and Print*

12. "How to Edit a Book," With a Friend—*Two Editions, Ebook and Print*

13. "How to Write Great Dialog"—*Two Editions, Ebook and Print*

14. "How to Market Your Book," Marketing 101–*Two Editions, Ebook and Print*

15. "Cover Design Bargain Bundle," Two for One, Includes #8 and #9–*Print Edition Only*

16. "Marketing Bargain Bundle," Two for One, Includes #14 and #6–*Print Edition Only*

17. "Book Marketing Bargain Bundle," Three for One, Includes #14, #6 and # 3-*Print Edition Only*

18. "Formatting Bargain Bundle," Two for One, Includes # 7 and # 11-*Print Edition Only*

19. "How to Register ISBNs & Copyrights" –*Two Editions, Ebook and Print*

20. "How to Get an Audible Version'" *for Your Book*–*Two Editions, Ebook and Print*

21. "How to Self-Publish" *Your Book*–*Two Editions, Ebook and Print* (Includes #11 and #20)

22. "How to Write Fiction" –*Two Editions, Ebook and Print*

23. "How to Create a Picture Book" – *Two Editions, Ebook and Print*

Links to all of these books can be found at

www.mercerpublications.com

BOOKS FROM MERCERPUBLICATIONS.

Links to all of these books can be found at
www.mercerpublications.com

<u>All novels are page-turners, complete stories in
themselves.</u>

Check out great reads, entertaining books

by Dorothy May Mercer

- **<u>The McBride Series of Action Novels,
  Starring Det. Lt. Michael J. McBride Jr.
  available in English and Spanish, ebook,
  print and Audible editions</u>**
- A Series for Those Looking for Good Clean
  Cop Stories. Now in English. And Spanish.

-

"Car oo6 Responding" Busy border cops. Mike
meets Juli
."The Cocaine Chase" Drug king-pin escapes
again.

"The Golden Coin" Illegal immigrants colide with violent cartels.

"The Cartel Wars" break out in the US. Mike proposes Juli.

"The Gang Bust" Mike wraps-up gangs & drug criminals. M & J wed.

Same as above in Spanish

"Unidad oo6 Respondiendo"

"La Casa di la Cocaina"

"El Immigrant e la Monada Dorada

"La Guerras Cartel"

"La Pandilla Busto

- **The Washington McBride Novels, Starring Senator Mike McBride, his wife Juliette, featuring his bodyguard, Cynthia Patterson. available in ebook, print and Audible editions**
- Author: Dorothy May Mercer

"the Fairfax Fix" Based on true story. H.S. girls recruited into prostitution ring. 4 disappear. Cops invstigate.

"the Arlington Alias" Investigative reporter, Juli McBride, exposes D.C. human trafficking ring.

s"<u>the Savage Surrogate</u>" Fran is kidnapped into slavery as surrogate mom. Juli searches world for her.

More from Dorothy May Mercer, author:

- **<u>The McBride Suspense/Romances, available in eBook, print and Audible editions</u>**

"<u>Fran and Max</u>" The Bungalow. Pregnant and hidden from the syndicate. Will they find her?

"<u>Cynthia and Dan,</u>" Cyber War. Terrorists attempt assassinate Pres with drones. "C" falls mysterious stranger.

"<u>Mary Beth and Sammy,</u>" Rolling Thunder. Dumb college kid joins gangs. Co-ed disappears. MB falls for handsome guy.

"<u>Nate" The Search</u> Father's search for long-lost daughter. Terrorists plot hi-tech multiple plane crashes.

"E-M-P Honeymoon" New bride blunders into terrorists plot. Can CIA & US Space Force save her?

Photo-Travel books by Dorothy May Mercer, author, and Dave Mercer, photographer:

- "Alaska and Back" With Dave and Dorothy.
- "Africa and Back" With Dave and Dorothy
- "Hawaii and Back," Vol. 1 Kauai" With Dave and Dorothy
- "Hawaii and Back," Vol 2, Maui, With Dave and Dorothy
- "Hawaii and Back," Vol 3, Oahu, With Dave and Dorothy
- "Hawaii and Back," Vol 4, Kauai Via SFO, With Dave and Dorothy
- "Niagara and Back," With Dave and Dorothy

More books by Dorothy May Mercer:

"Leon and Esther," an historical Christian love story. Perfect for the Advent season, or anytime.

"Stories I Haven't Told," an auto-biography. Barefoot Depression baby becomes multi-millionaire CEO.

Various Author's Books published by Mercer Publications & Ministries, Inc.:

- "Let's Talk" a Black/White Dialog in the US & the UK
- "Short & Fun Stories" Vol. 1 & 2, by fourteen authors.
- "Stormy Affair," a Romance, by Netty Ejike
- "Sensual Bond," 5 Part Saga Series, by Netty Ejike
- "He Called Her Hat," That Tough Little Lady, Amusing Historical Biography, by Myron C. McDonald
- "Notes from John," Messages from Beyond, by Marcia McMahon
- "Remember How Much I Love You," Romantic Action Suspense, by Dale L. Williams, M.D.
- "The Inheritance from Hell," True Drama, by R.D. Margot
- "Ascension Teachings," With Archangel Michael, by Marcia McMahon
- "Gems" a collection of dream-time peotry, by Nancy Calumet, illustrated by Dorothy May Mercer
- "Without from Within" a poetry collection, by Ron Shaw

New in Audible Book (Talking Books) Versions:

The McBride Series of Action Novels, Starring Det. Lt. Michael J. McBride Jr. in English & Spanish Audible version:

"Car 006 Responding"

"The Cocaine Chase"

"The Golden Coin"

"The Cartel Wars

"The Gang Bust"

Action Novels in Audible version:

"The Fairfax Fix"

"The Arlington Alias"

"The Savage Surrogate"

Action/Romantic Suspense Novels in Audible versions:

"Fran and Max, The Bungalow

"Cynthia and Dan" *Cyber War*

"Mary Beth and Sammy," *Rolling Thunder*

"Leon and Esther"

"E-M-P Honeymoon" Kelly & Tom

Non-Fiction in Audible version:"

"Let's Talk" a Black/White Dialog in the US & the UK

Not many folks will take the trouble to post a review, and even fewer will bother to copy and paste it in other marketplaces. You are truly one in a million! Three Cheers!

- If you purchased this book, I know you will not "return" it for a refund. Sometimes, customers do so, perhaps unaware that it puts a black mark on the author's record. Amazon keeps track of these things.

- If you used the Amazon library option, and borrowed this book, you may return it, now, and borrow it again, anytime. You may even buy it. Whee!

While you are there, please consider buying/borrowing another book by Dorothy May Mercer. Or, you may consider the Want-to-Buy option and put several books on your "Add to

Wish List." Amazon notices everything! Besides, this list makes a good suggestion for your next birthday or anniversary wish list.

Another good option is the "Give as a Gift." Amazon sends a beautiful gift card to the recipient. You can add your own special message. Easy-Peezy.

Two easy ways to find all of the Dorothy May Mercer books:

1. Go to www.MercerPublications.com for links.

Tip: Look at the "How to For You" menu for 23 helpful books for authors and indie publishers.

2. Go to any Amazon site and search for Dorothy May Mercer.

Tip: There are seven + Amazon pages for her books. The control at the bottom of the first page will navigate you to any page of her books.

Check out the latest at:

http://www.MercerPublications.com

Facebook: Savage Surrogate

https://www.facebook.com/SavageSurrogate?_rdr=p

Blog:

http://mikemcbridenovels.blogspot.com/

Twitter: DorothyMMercer

Thank you for purchasing this "How to For You" Series. We hope you enjoyed and found at least one helpful tip. Please encourage other writers by posting a short, positive review on the Amazon or other site where you purchased this book. Go to one or all of the following Amazon pages:

Amazon USA www.amazon.com

Amazon United Kingdom www.amazon.co.uk

Amazon Canada www.amazon.ca

Amazon Brazil www.amazon.br

Amazon Mexico www.amazon.com.mx

Amazon France www.amazon.fr

Amazon Italy www.amazon.com.it

Amazon Denmark www.amazon.de

Amazon India www.amazon.in

Amazon Australia www.amazon.com.au

Thanks, Again.

See you soon, in another book.

Dorothy May Mercer, Author Extraordinaire

Have a wonderful day!

For prices and ordering information please copy the address below:

www.MercerPublications.com

Still have questions? Comments?

Write Dorothy at

info@mercerpublications.com.

We absolutely love to hear from our readers.